Historical Biographies

DiscoverRoo

An Imprint of Pop!
popbooksonline.com

JIM THORPE

Versatile Athlete and Olympian

by Grace Hansen

WELCOME TO DiscoverRoo!

This book is filled with videos, puzzles, games, and more! Scan the QR codes* while you read, or visit the website below to make this book pop.

https://popbooksonline.com/thorpe

abdobooks.com
Published by Pop!, a division of ABDO, PO Box 398166, Minneapolis, Minnesota 55439.

Printed in the United States of America, North Mankato, Minnesota.

102022
012023

THIS BOOK CONTAINS RECYCLED MATERIALS

Cover Photo: Getty Image Collection; Shutterstock Images

Interior Photos: Getty Image Collection; Shutterstock Images; Cumberland County Historical Society; Library of Congress; Everett Collection; AP Images

Editor: Elizabeth Andrews

Series Designers: Laura Graphenteen; Neil Klinepier

Library of Congress Control Number: 2022941247

Publisher's Cataloging-in-Publication Data

Names: Hansen, Grace, author.

Title: Jim Thorpe: versatile athlete and olympian / by Grace Hansen

Description: Minneapolis, Minnesota : Pop!, 2023 | Series: Historical biographies | Includes online resources and index.

Identifiers: ISBN 9781098243395 (lib. bdg.) | ISBN 9781098244095 (ebook)

Subjects: LCSH: Thorpe, Jim, 1887-1953--Juvenile literature. | Football players--Biography--Juvenile literature. | American football--Juvenile literature. | Olympics athletes--Biography--Juvenile literature. | Indian athletes--Biography--Juvenile literature.

Classification: DDC 796.092 [B]--dc23

*Scanning QR codes requires a web-enabled smart device with a QR code reader app and a camera.

TABLE OF CONTENTS

CHAPTER 1

BRIGHT PATH

James Francis Thorpe was born a twin on May 28, 1887, in what would later be the state of Oklahoma. Jim and his brother Charlie were of both American Indian and European **ancestry**. Their mother was of the Potawatomi Nation. Their father was of the Sac and Fox Nation.

WATCH A VIDEO HERE!

When Jim was born, no one could have guessed that he would go on to star for many different teams, including baseball's New York Giants.

The Sac and Fox Nation is located in Oklahoma.

The boys were raised Sac and Fox. Jim's parents also gave him the name Wa-tho-huk, meaning "Bright Path" in the Sac and Fox language. In Jim's case, lighting a way forward would be a theme throughout his life.

Jim and Charlie grew up with their older siblings on a farm. Jim was small, but strong and naturally athletic. The boys loved playing outside and learning new skills, like tracking wild animals and roping and riding horses. But before the twins' ninth birthday, Charlie became ill and passed away. Losing his twin brother and best friend was devastating for Jim. Not long after, Jim's mother died too. Feeling lost, Jim was forced to pave a path all his own.

CHAPTER 2

THE GREATEST ATHLETE IN THE WORLD

Jim's first step forward was enrolling at the **Carlisle Indian Industrial School** in Pennsylvania in 1903. One day in 1907, Jim joined the open tryouts for the school's track and field team. Without ever practicing, Jim leaped 5-feet,

LEARN MORE HERE!

9-inches (1.8m) off the ground to break the school's record for high jump. This fantastic feat began his athletic career.

Thorpe posing in his track and field uniform for the Carlisle Indian Industrial School.

The Carlisle Indian Industrial School was small. But with Thorpe, it would become an athletic powerhouse known especially for its football program. The football team was led by Coach Glenn "Pop" Warner. The coach knew Jim would

Thorpe was a talent on the gridiron too.

be a great addition to the team. However, allowing the school's track star to play football would be a risk. But Thorpe quickly proved that his worth on the **gridiron** outweighed any risk of injury.

In 1909, Thorpe decided to take a break from school to play semiprofessional baseball in North Carolina. Little did Jim know, this would affect his future athletic accomplishments.

DID YOU KNOW?

Thorpe had a little-known career in basketball. He considered playing professional hockey too!

Thorpe (right) *stands with his teammates and Pop Warner* (middle).

Jim rejoined Pop and the football team at Carlisle in 1911 and 1912. Together, they **upset** teams such as Harvard, Brown, and the US Military Academy. In fact, those Carlisle football teams are still considered the best of their time. In the 1912 season, Thorpe alone scored 25 touchdowns and 198 points, and was named **All-American**. The team went 12-1-1.

Thorpe surprised the world when he took his talents to the global stage. In the summer of 1912, Jim represented the United States at the Olympics in Stockholm, Sweden. He won gold medals in both the **pentathlon** and the **decathlon**.

Thorpe poses at the 1912 Summer Olympics in Stockholm, Sweden.

King Gustav V of Sweden approached Jim at the closing ceremonies, shook his hand, and said, "You, sir, are the greatest athlete in the world." Six months later, the International Olympic Committee would strip Jim of his medals for his time playing semiprofessional baseball.

ALIASES

Thorpe did as other college athletes had done. He earned money playing sports in the summer months. In 1912, the Olympics had strict rules against its participating athletes ever being paid for playing a sport. Jim did not know this rule and played as himself. Other college athletes played under made up names.

Jim could only move forward and prove that he was in fact one of the greatest athletes in the world. On April 14, 1913, Thorpe made his Major League Baseball debut with the New York Giants! The same year, the athlete also

Thorpe played outfield for the New York Giants.

began a professional football career. In 1915, Thorpe was making $250, nearly $7,000 in today's dollars, per game with the Canton Bulldogs. Before his arrival, the team was averaging just 1,200 fans per game. But 8,000 came to cheer on Jim from the stands at his first game, showing he was worth the big payday.

Jim would even go on to coach football from the college level to the pros. It was as if there was nothing left for him to conquer. But Jim took on Hollywood next.

CHAPTER 3

BIG SCREEN STAR

The Great Depression (1929–1939) was a hard time for almost every person in the United States and around the world. Having retired from professional sports, Thorpe needed to plan his next step and make money.

Thorpe's athletic build and American Indian background allowed him to fill

COMPLETE AN ACTIVITY HERE!

Thorpe (right) *on the set of* My Pal, the King *in 1932.*

movie roles that few others could. Jim was first cast to play Chief Black Crow in *Battling with Buffalo Bill* in 1931. Thorpe went on to have many notable parts and would appear in more than 70 films. As the demand for Thorpe in the movie industry grew, he did not keep all the glory for himself.

CHAPTER 4

CAREGIVER

In 1935 alone, Jim appeared in 19 movies. He received many calls about fellow American Indians looking for work. Thorpe was frustrated by people of different backgrounds being cast in American Indian roles. So, Jim cofounded the Indian

EXPLORE LINKS HERE!

Center. It was a place where American Indians from around the United States could come to stay in California. Thorpe helped them find housing and work in the television and film industries.

Men and women from 18 different nations meet in 1932 to protest representation in Hollywood.

It was during his time in Hollywood that Thorpe earned the nickname Akapamata, the Sac and Fox word for "caregiver." And it's no wonder. Thorpe put great care into everything he tried. And he put even more care into people, especially the American Indian community. Jim wanted them to have equal pay and rights, and for their stories to be told.

"I am no more proud of my career as an athlete than I am of the fact that I am a direct descendant of that noble warrior [Chief Black Hawk]."

Thorpe with his sons Phil (left) *and Billy at their Inglewood, California, home.*

CHAPTER 5

DEATH AND LEGACY

Much of Thorpe's later years were spent helping others. However, Jim also dealt with issues that lead to health problems. Jim died of heart failure on March 28, 1953, at the age of 65.

Thorpe is often remembered as one of the greatest athletes of the 20th century. But he was much more than that. He overcame many hardships

Jim setting the pace for a junior Olympics event in Chicago in 1948.

throughout his lifetime. And he did it all while also representing the Sac and Fox Nation and all American Indian people.

Thorpe is greeted on a Florida football field by a group of American Indians from a nearby reservation.

At the time of the 1912 Olympics, not all American Indians were even considered citizens of the United States. Many believe that Jim's rightly earned gold medals were striped from him because of his background. Years after his death, the Jim Thorpe Foundation was started. It gained support from US Congress to reinstate Thorpe as a two-time Olympic champion. And in October 1982, the International Olympic Committee approved the reinstatement. Jim Thorpe was once again an Olympic gold medalist.

★ HALL OF FAMER ★

College Football Hall of Fame – Inducted in 1951
Pro Football Hall of Fame – Inducted in 1963
National Track and Field Hall of Fame – Inducted in 1975
US Olympic Hall of Fame – Inducted in 1983
National Native American Hall of Fame – Inducted in 2018

IMPORTANT DATES

MAY 28, 1887
James Francis Thorpe is born to part American Indian parents in what is present-day Oklahoma.

1903
Thorpe begins attending the Carlisle Indian Industrial School where he later stars on the track and field and football teams.

1912 SUMMER OLYMPICS
Thorpe competes at the Olympic Games in Stockholm where he takes home the gold in both the decathlon and pentathlon.

FEBRUARY 1, 1913

Thorpe signs a three-year contract with the New York Giants Major League Baseball team.

MARCH 28, 1953

Thorpe passes away at the age of 65.

1931

Jim appears in his first Hollywood movie. He goes on to act and star in countless others.

MAKING CONNECTIONS

TEXT-TO-SELF

What do you think Jim Thorpe's most important achievement was in his lifetime?

TEXT-TO-TEXT

Have you read any other books about Jim Thorpe? Did you learn any new information from those books?

TEXT-TO-WORLD

Can you think of any other people in history who devoted their lives to helping their communities?

GLOSSARY

All-American — chosen as one of the best players in the United States in a particular sport at a particular time.

ancestry — line of descent; one's family background.

Carlisle Indian Industrial School — (1879-1918) the first government-run boarding school for American Indians. Schools like this striped people of all Nations of their customs, culture, and heritage. However, Carlisle is also remembered for its impressive athletic teams, internationally-known band, and notable graduates who went on to work in activism.

decathlon — an athletic contest made up of ten different track and field events.

gridiron — another name for a football field.

pentathlon — a five-event contest in the Olympic games in which each competitor must ride horseback cross-country, run cross-country, swim, fence, and shoot a pistol.

upset — to win when expected to lose.

INDEX

DiscoverRoo!

ONLINE RESOURCES

This book is filled with videos, puzzles, games, and more! Scan the QR codes* while you read, or visit the website below to make this book pop.

https://popbooksonline.com/thorpe

*Scanning QR codes requires a web-enabled smart device with a QR code reader app and a camera.